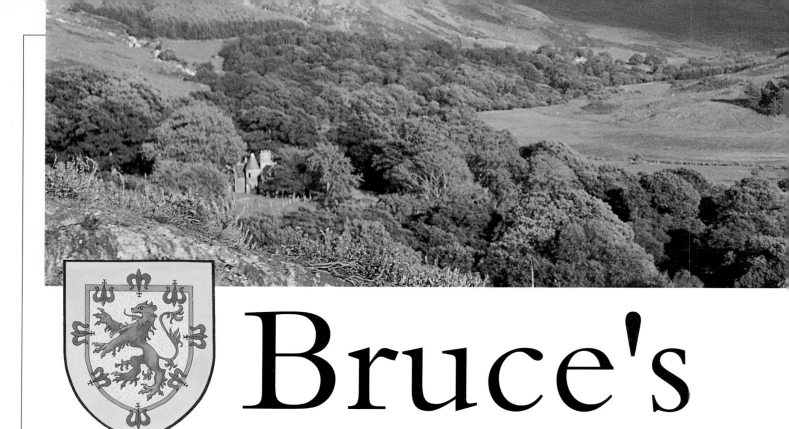

# Bruce's

Cover picture: Statue of Robert Bruce at Bannockburn.
Inside cover picture: The Pass of Brander, Argyll.
Title page picture: Bruce's Stone at Glen Trool.
First published in 1994 by Wayland (Publishers) Ltd,
61 Western Road, Hove, East Sussex BN3 1JD,
England.
© Copyright 1994 Wayland (Publishers) Ltd.
British Library Cataloguing in Publication Data

Spankie, Mari
  Bruce's Scotland
  I. Title
  941.102

ISBN 0-7502-1232-2

Consultants: Donald Gunn, Education Officer for BBC
Scotland, and Richard Dargie, Lecturer in History at
Moray House Institute of Education in Edinburgh.
Editor: Joanna Bentley
Book design and typesetting: Pardoe Blacker Limited
Printed and bound by B.P.C. Paulton Books, Great
Britain

## Picture acknowledgements
The publishers wish to thank the following for providing the illustrations in this book: British Library 17; The Master
and Fellows of Corpus Christi College, Cambridge 15, 34; Crown copyright/By permission of the Controller of Her
Majesty's Stationery Office 21 (bottom), 39; Cumbria Record Office 19; Donald Gunn 30, 31; Historic Scotland 13
(both), 27, 28, 37 (left), 39; National Galleries of Scotland/Scoular 41; © The Trustees of the National Museums of
Scotland 29, 35; By permission of the Duke of Roxburghe/National Library of Scotland 7 (top); Scottish Record
Office 38; Still Moving Picture Company 7 (bottom, A Burgess), 22 (left, K Paterson), 40 (Alasdair Smith); Wayland
Picture Library 18, 37 (right); By courtesy of the Dean and Chapter of Westminster 21 (top); David Williams Picture
Library 12, 16 (bottom).
Artwork by: Peter Bull 6, 8, 10, 22-3, 24-5, 30, 33, 34; Chris Ryley 9, 14-15, 20, 25, 26, 32.
Thanks to Professor Charles W J Withers for the languages map references on page 6.

# Scotland

# Contents

# Scotland: many Languages, one Nation

Robert Bruce was born on 11 July 1274 at Turnberry Castle on the Ayrshire coast. He was the eldest of a large family. He lived in the Middle Ages and Scotland was very different then. Several languages were spoken. As Bruce grew up he would come across Gaelic from his mother's people, Norman-French from his father and *Inglis* in parts of southern Scotland and the towns.

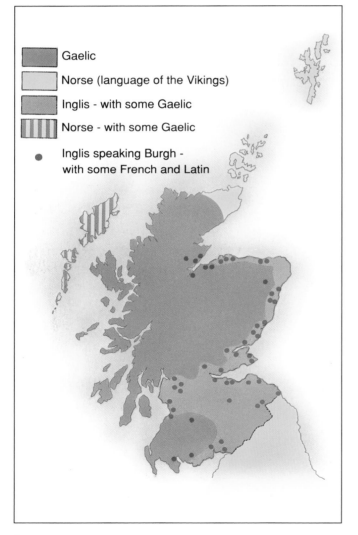

**Legend:**
- Gaelic
- Norse (language of the Vikings)
- Inglis – with some Gaelic
- Norse – with some Gaelic
- • Inglis speaking Burgh – with some French and Latin

## Gaelic

Since the time of Kenneth Macalpin, who was King of Scots from 843 to 860, Celtic culture in Scotland had been strong and growing. It was built on the most common language, Gaelic, and reached to the north of England. There were also Celtic links with Ireland and the Isle of Man. Family ties were very important to the Celtic peoples in the Middle Ages.

## Inglis

The Norman Conquest of England in 1066 forced some Saxons to flee north. This helped spread their language, Inglis, in southern Scotland. From around 1100, it gradually took over from Gaelic as the main language of the people in lowland areas. Many people now call this language Scots, the name the Inglis-speakers used for Gaelic in the Middle Ages.

## Norman-French

Before David I became King of Scots in 1124 he spent many years at the Anglo-Norman court and at his estates in England. He was interested in the modern, Norman ideas.

**This map of Scotland shows where the most common languages were spoken by the people around 1300.**

King David invited some Norman knights to come to Scotland. These knights helped him to keep control of his kingdom because they were good soldiers. This began the Norman influence in Scotland. They brought their language, French to Scotland. The knights gave the king homage, an oath of loyalty and a promise to fight when he needed them. The king gave the knights lands in return.

Growing up in the following century, the young Robert Bruce knew both the Celtic and the Norman ways of life. He grew up knowing the importance of kinship (family ties) from the family's Celtic earldom of Carrick.

David I and his grandson Malcolm IV, from a charter giving lands to Kelso Abbey in 1159. Charters were written in Latin, the language of the Church and government.

Motte and bailey castles were found in most mainland areas of Scotland, except the north west. In 1305 a Norman-Scottish family replaced the wooden castle at Duffus with this stone castle and wall.

He was also a Norman lord, trained in knightly combat. His family was one of the most powerful families in both England and Scotland.

Like the Bruce family, many people in Scotland at this time came from a mixture of cultures. Bruce was able to use this variety to build a stronger nation after he became king.

# A Kingdom at Peace

Robert Bruce grew up in a country at peace under King Alexander III. Bruce's family had built strong, stone castles to show their wealth and importance in both Scotland and England. They had many relations and knights who paid homage to them in return for land.

Nine out of ten people lived in small farming communities. These grew round a landlord's hall or castle. Some estates had between ten and twenty touns paying rent or goods to the landlord. These were known as shires or baronies. The landlords were called barons, men who were responsible for a barony. Each barony had its own parish church. In the Highlands these communities were led by local chiefs.

Below: A typical farming estate around a landlord's castle.

A knight in armour.

## Population

- It is estimated that the population of Scotland was nearly 1 million by the year 1300.
- England's population was between 5 and 6 million at this time.
- At least 90 per cent of Scots lived in small rural communities.
- Half the population lived north of the line between the Rivers Clyde and Jay.

## Money

- Scottish money was worth the same as English money.
- Scotland had 30 - 45 million silver pennies being used.

The farmers in each toun shared the arable ground on the sloping hillsides to grow crops. They grew barley, oats and a little wheat. They kept cattle and sheep, selling the wool and hides. They did not know how to drain the flatter, wetter ground but it was sometimes used as pasture for the cattle.

Being a knight was an expensive business. They needed horses, armour and weapons. Knights were soldiers not farmers. Their money came from their tenants who paid them rent and fines for breaking the law. The tenants also worked the knight's own fields, called his demesne. Knights were expected to protect their tenants and to take their men to fight for the king.

When there were wars the men of the estate made up the infantry and bowmen of the king's army. In the Highlands and the west, this service to the king was sometimes paid in galleys and oarsmen instead of horsemen.

# Trade and the Burghs

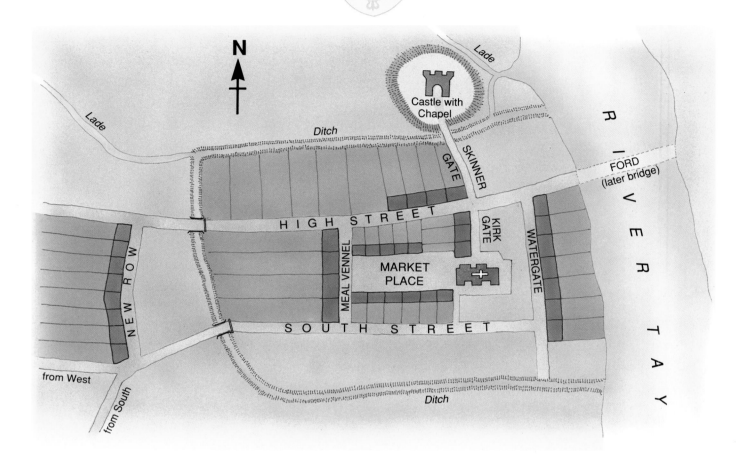

A plan of St John's Town (which we now call Perth).

The earliest burghs in Scotland were set up by kings and called royal burghs. Later, barons set up burghs around their castles. They were called 'burghs of barony'. The Bruce family would have known several of Scotland's burghs well. The family had set up their own burgh at Annan.

Burgh laws said what was allowed in the town. The people living in the town had many privileges. Only burghs were allowed to hold markets and fairs. Farmers had to sell what they grew at their local town. This kept the prices down for the townspeople and encouraged traders and craftsmen to live in towns. The nobles made money by setting tolls. These were collected from the traders as they entered the burgh gates.

Alexander III's reign (1249-1286) was a prosperous time in Scotland. The towns and the country depended on each other.

The country provided the raw materials, usually wool and hides, and food for the townspeople. The craftsmen in the burghs made goods for sale such as shoes, saddles and woven cloth. Guilds in the towns were set up to control the quality and prices of these goods. They were powerful and the burgesses who ran them were part of the king's government.

The most important burghs were on the east coast, like Aberdeen in the north and Berwick in the south. Their merchants exported hides, wool and timber to Europe and England. Berwick, with a population of around 6,000 people, was the richest town in Scotland. Merchants there exported the fine wool from the Border Abbeys and brought in luxury goods such as wine and spices.

Burghs were small, dirty, dangerous places. Water came from wells and rubbish was left lying around. This could lead to disease. The wooden houses often caught fire and a whole town could easily burn down.

**This picture shows all that remains of Roxburghe Castle.**

# The Scottish Church in the Middle Ages

Scotland did well in bringing together two different traditions of Christian worship: the old Celtic Church and the Roman Catholic Church. The ties with the Roman Church had grown since King David I (1084–1153) had brought Roman Catholic churchmen to the country. In time, Roman Catholic traditions became the most common. By 1174 the Pope, head of the Roman Catholic Church, recognized the Scottish Church as a 'special daughter' of Rome. This gave Scotland's churchmen many important links with Europe.

St Columba (Columcille) landed on Iona in 563. The island was the centre of the Celtic Church for hundreds of years. Early kings of Scots were buried in the Rellig Odhrain (the Graveyard of the Kings).

The Pope also recognized the ancient Celtic Church and its saints, such as Columcille (Columba). The Celtic Church survived in the time of Bruce and was known as the Culdees (Celi De means servants of God in Gaelic). Members of the Celtic Church were often missionaries and they led very simple lives.

David I encouraged the Roman Church to grow by granting charters to religious orders. This meant that the king gave them land and special permission for monasteries and abbeys to be set up. There were different religious orders, but monks were all expected to live a life of prayer, study and manual work. The running of large estates made the abbeys wealthy.

Right: Melrose Abbey was one of Scotland's wealthiest abbeys. Its wool was sent to Roxburghe, then on to Berwick for export.

Below: The ruins of Kelso Abbey are all that is left today of the royal power base in southern Scotland.

By 1300 Scotland had thirty abbeys, twenty-seven priories, nine nunneries and twenty friaries, as well as a network of parish churches covering the country.

The Church linked Scottish communities but it also linked Scotland with the outside world. Younger sons of noble families often worked in the Church. Bruce's brother, Alexander, was a clergyman. Bishops, the Church leaders, were powerful. They were part of the king's government. The Chancellor of the kingdom was usually a churchman. He was responsible for the king's written and legal business. The Scottish Church fought against the English taking over their church and their country.

13

# 1286, King Alexander III

Alexander III was King of Scots from 1249 to 1286. He was a strong king, and for most of his reign Scotland was a peaceful, successful kingdom. The Celtic influence was still strong. Links with England were good, partly because Alexander's wife was the sister of the English king, Edward I. Edward I had already invaded Ireland and Wales and made them provinces of England, but he seemed to be a friend to Scotland and her king.

Alexander III said to Edward I in October 1278:

'I become your man for the lands which I hold of you in the kingdom of England for which I owe homage, saving [except for] my kingdom.'

When homage for Scotland was asked for, he replied;

'No one has a right to homage for my kingdom of Scotland save God alone, and I hold it only of God.'

All was well until Alexander's wife and sons died unexpectedly and the 45-year-old king no longer had a son to be king after him. He married again at Jedburgh Abbey, where the ceremony was spoiled, it is said, by skeletons joining in the dancing. Some people thought this was a warning of trouble ahead for the country. His second wife, Yolande of Dreux, was young and beautiful.

On 12 March 1286 the king sat in Edinburgh Castle eating with his lords. It was a stormy day and getting late. His thoughts turned to his wife in their

manor house at Kinghorn, twenty miles
away by bad roads and a ferry across the
River Forth. In spite of the protests of
his barons and others he tried to reach
home that wild night. He crossed the
Forth safely, lost his companions in the
dark and was found the next morning,
dead at the bottom of a cliff. This tragic
accident left Scotland without a king. It
led to Edward I of England trying to gain
control of Scotland, and began more
than a hundred years of conflict between
Scotland and England.

# The Kingdom without a King

When Alexander III died his granddaughter Margaret was to become Queen of Scots. She was young and lived with her father, the King of Norway. King Edward I of England began to arrange a marriage between Margaret and his son. This would bring Scotland under his control.

In Scotland everyday life carried on. The nobles and churchmen chose six Guardians to govern the country. The clever choice of Guardians showed that they knew Scotland was in a dangerous situation without a king. The six men had influence in different parts of the country. Three supported the Bruce family, who had a claim to the throne, and three supported the Baliol–Comyn family, who also had a strong claim to the throne. This kept both families working together for the country.

It was not until 1290 that Margaret of Norway began the journey to Scotland. But she became ill and died on Orkney. This left Scotland with no direct heir to the throne and Edward I was disappointed.

Thirteen important lords now claimed the throne. The Scottish lords went to Edward I and asked for help to make the best choice.

Above: The Guardians of Scotland did not use a king's seal. Their seal showed St Andrew, patron saint of Scotland.

At Norham Castle in 1291 the Scots politely refused to accept Edward I as a superior to the King of Scots.

16

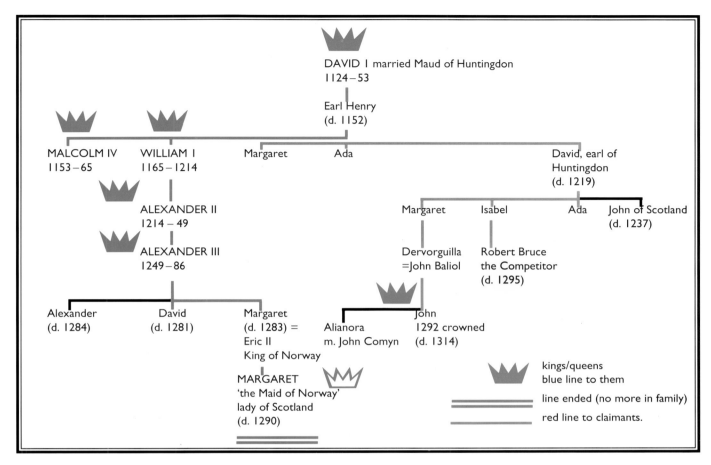

DAVID I married Maud of Huntingdon
1124–53

Earl Henry
(d. 1152)

MALCOLM IV
1153–65

WILLIAM I
1165–1214

Margaret

Ada

David, earl of
Huntingdon
(d. 1219)

ALEXANDER II
1214–49

Margaret

Isabel

Ada

John of Scotland
(d. 1237)

ALEXANDER III
1249–86

Dervorguilla
=John Baliol

Robert Bruce
the Competitor
(d. 1295)

Alexander
(d. 1284)

David
(d. 1281)

Margaret
(d. 1283) =
Eric II
King of Norway

Alianora
m. John Comyn

John
1292 crowned
(d. 1314)

MARGARET
'the Maid of Norway'
lady of Scotland
(d. 1290)

kings/queens
blue line to them

line ended (no more in family)

red line to claimants.

They made it very clear to Edward in the letters they sent that Scotland was an independent nation. Edward brought his army to the border when he came to judge what was called 'The Great Cause'.

Two Scottish nobles had the best claim. One was Robert Bruce's grandfather, sometimes known as The Competitor, and the other was John Baliol, head of the Baliol-Comyn family. Before Edward would choose, the two men had to agree to accept his decision. Edward chose John Baliol. He was crowned at the end of November 1292 and paid homage to Edward at Christmas in Newcastle. Baliol was warned to govern justly or his Lord Superior might have to interfere.

King John Baliol pays homage to England's Edward I.

# England's Warrior King

Edward I was a clever man who used the law to get what he wanted, but he was also a very good army commander. He had already defeated the Welsh and kept them under control by building strong, stone castles. His soldiers lived in these and ruled Wales for him.

Edward commanded a powerful army, made up of heavy cavalry, archers and foot soldiers. English nobles and knights with their own men-at-arms rode heavy horses called destriers. These horses were like the tanks of today. Scotland did not have many heavy war horses.

The knights wore chain mail to protect themselves. This was covered with a tunic showing their family coat of arms. Their weapons were a long lance and a mace or battleaxe for close combat. If they were captured in battle they expected to be looked after, ransomed and then set free. The knights were the most important part of the English army.

In Scotland the foot soldiers fought for the king when he called for them. This was called forinsec, or Scots service. Each man had a helmet, a padded coat to protect him against arrows, and chain mail gloves to hold his 3.6-metre-long spear.

**Opposite: The Scots attack Edward I's Carlisle Castle.**

**Left: The coronation of England's King Edward I in 1272.**

ꝏꞇ ad Cuutatem ꝛ

He also had a sword, axe or dirk (dagger) for close fighting and carried a targe (a shield made of animal skins). Both countries had archers but the English longbow was a more powerful weapon.

When John Baliol became king there had been no fighting in Scotland for almost thirty years and the country was not ready for war. Many of the noble families had lands in both England and Scotland. It was hard to choose whom to be loyal to when Edward showed that he wanted Scotland to be part of his kingdom.

The Bruces found it hard to accept Baliol as king and the family did not give up hope of one of them becoming King of Scots one day. They admired Edward I, who had treated them well in the past and given them important castles to look after.

# King John Baliol and the Sack of Berwick

Edward I tried to use his position as Lord Superior of Scotland to force King John to do as he wished. He treated the king as if he was one of his nobles and Scotland as if it was a part of England.

In his three years as king, John did not work alone. The churchmen worked with him to protect Scotland's rights as an independent nation. Most of the lords in the parliaments supported him, too. Much of the work of the country carried on smoothly in spite of King Edward's claims and interference.

When Edward went to war with France in 1294 he sent a message to Scotland demanding that the king, the earls and barons take their men to fight for him in France. The Scots refused to go but they knew how dangerous this was. They made an alliance (agreement to help each other) with France and King John called up his army to gather close to the English border in March 1296.

Edward I destroyed Berwick to make the Scots accept his rule.

Edward punished the Scots for rebelling against him by attacking their richest town, Berwick. His soldiers killed, looted and burned the town for three days. Traders from overseas were slaughtered and Edward ordered that the dead be left in the streets to rot. In Europe people were shocked by Edward's actions. In only seventeen days the Scottish army was defeated.

Edward set up his headquarters in Berwick and made the Earl of Surrey Governor of Scotland. The English king then marched north. He seized government papers, the crown jewels, holy relics like the Black Rood (cross) of St Margaret and the coronation stone from Scone (the Stone of Destiny). In July, at Montrose Castle, King John was stripped of his tunic (showing the royal coat of arms), his hood and his knight's belt. This was a punishment for knights found guilty of treason, not for a defeated king. From this event comes Baliol's nickname 'Toom Tabard' or empty jacket. After being shamed in this way John was forced to give up the crown.

All landowners were called to Berwick to pay homage to Edward if they wished to keep their land. In August, 1,500 landowners signed a document promising loyalty to the English king. This document came to be called 'The Ragman Roll'. Scotland no longer had a king and English soldiers held many important castles in Scotland.

Left: The Coronation Chair in Westminster Abbey. The Stone of Destiny is still in place beneath this throne.

Below: By signing the Ragman Roll, 1500 Scots landowners promised loyalty to Edward I.

# The Rise of William Wallace and Andrew Murray

When Edward I returned to England, the Scots turned against the men he had left to rule them. The nobles and clergy did not fight Edward openly, but there was widespread resistance. In July 1297 Cressingham, Edward's tax gatherer for Scotland, wrote to London, complaining that the Scots would not pay their taxes:

> 'Not one of the sheriffs, bailiffs or officials of the Lord King appointed within that kingdom can at this time raise a penny of the revenues of their bailiwicks, on account of a multitude of different perils which daily and continually threaten them.'

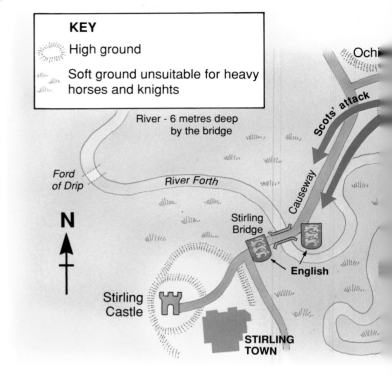

The Battle of Stirling Bridge, 1297.

Two young men led Scotland's organized resistance: in the north, Andrew Murray of Petty, a baron's son, and in the south, William Wallace, the second son of a knight from Elderslie, near Paisley. By August of the same year, Murray and Wallace had joined forces. A well-armed, experienced English army marched towards Stirling to put down the Scots' revolt.

The Wallace Monument stands on Abbey Craig, where Wallace commanded the Battle of Stirling Bridge.

# Battle of Stirling Bridge
# 11 September 1297

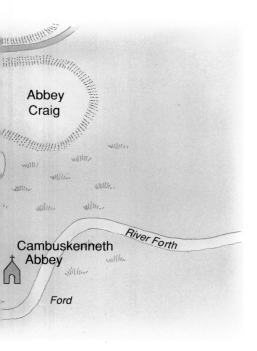

The armies met at Stirling on opposite banks of the River Forth. The English occupied Stirling Castle. Few Scottish nobles were ready to fight alongside their fellow Scots. The English were confident, but Wallace would not surrender. He said:

> '...we are not here to make peace but to do battle to defend ourselves and to liberate our kingdom.'

The Scots held a strong position. The English had to cross the river to reach them. The English leaders argued about how to fight the battle. Cressingham said:

> 'Don't waste more of the King's time and money. Cross the river now by the bridge.'

An English knight said:

> 'Send a force of knights and men to secure the ford. They can attack the Scots from behind and let the rest of our army cross the bridge.'

The Earl of Surrey chose to cross by the narrow, wooden bridge. The knights on horseback went first. To their surprise the Scots attacked. The knights were unable to move and the bridge was jammed with horses and men. Many soldiers drowned trying to escape. The English were defeated.

Wallace and Murray wrote to German merchants telling them it was now safe to visit Scottish ports again:

> 'for the kingdom of Scotland, God be thanked, has been recovered by war from the power of the English.'

This painting is of the Battle of Stirling Bridge, by William Hole.

# Wallace is Defeated

The success at Stirling Bridge brought hope to the Scots. Wallace and Murray were appointed joint Guardians of Scotland. For Wallace this was a great honour. He had been knighted around this time but he did not have the high status of the great lords and landowners. This made it difficult for him to be accepted by many of the noble families. However, he and Murray did govern Scotland with the help of the church and some of the nobles. Unfortunately, Andrew Murray died a few months after the battle of Stirling Bridge and Wallace became Scotland's only Guardian.

Edward I's hatred of the Scots, and of Wallace in particular, grew. He gathered a huge army of 4,000 cavalry and 25,000 foot soldiers, including conscripts from Wales.

'Bas agus Buaid - Death and Victory'. Wallace inspired the Scots people and Robert Bruce to fight for freedom, even after his death.

Right: The Battle of Falkirk was a disaster for the Scots. The English had much better weapons, which helped lead to their victory.

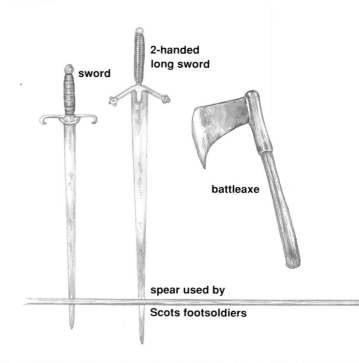

sword

2-handed long sword

battleaxe

spear used by Scots footsoldiers

A schiltrom was used for defence against knights on horseback.

In 1298 the Scots and English armies met at Falkirk. The archers in the English army poured arrows into the tightly packed, slow-moving schiltroms. The Scots were defeated. Wallace escaped, forced to flee by his supporters. He gave up the guardianship but kept on organizing resistance to the English.

Many of the lords who had fought under Wallace paid homage to Edward. John Comyn, nephew of Baliol, and Robert Bruce, grandson of Bruce the Competitor, were among these.

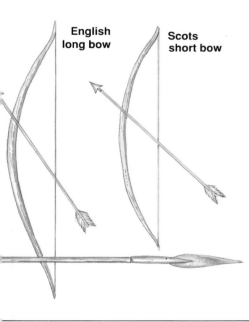

**English long bow**

**Scots short bow**

Between 1298 and 1304 Edward brought armies to Scotland to show his strength. He besieged castles still held by the Scots. He even refused to accept the surrender of Stirling Castle until his latest siege engine, 'Warwolf', was given a day to show what damage it could do.

Wallace stayed loyal to King John. It is likely he was sent on special missions abroad. In spite of all Edward's power he was not captured until 1305. He was sent to London to stand trial for treason and was treated as an outlaw. Wallace did not see how he could be charged with treason as his country was at war with England and he had never paid homage to Edward. Nevertheless he was found guilty. He was dragged through the streets, hanged, taken down alive, tortured, beheaded and his body cut into four. The pieces were sent back to Scotland to try to frighten the people.

# Murder: a step to the Throne

By 1306 the Scots had been at war with England for ten years. Most lords and churchmen had taken an oath of allegiance to Edward rather than lose their lands or their lives. The English king thought Scotland had finally been defeated. He did not understand the determination of the ordinary people to be free.

Nobles, too, wanted freedom. One of them had fought along with Wallace, had sworn allegiance to Edward and had watched and learned. He was Robert Bruce, Earl of Carrick and Lord of Annandale. He had inherited his family's claim to the throne and his grandfather's ambition to be king. He thought that the people would rise against Edward once more if they had a strong king. He was ready to be that king.

On 10 February 1306 the English were holding a law court in Dumfries Castle. Two of Scotland's most powerful young men met in the nearby Greyfriars Kirk.

John Comyn, Lord of Badenoch, was a patriot and his uncle was John Baliol, the last king. He was head of a powerful group of nobles and churchmen. Historians think Robert Bruce set up the meeting to ask for Comyn's support in a revolt against the English. Bruce and Bishop Lamberton of St Andrews were secretly working together but they knew they needed the Comyn family's support.

Unfortunately, Bruce and Comyn did not trust or like each other. Both were hot tempered and they began to argue while they were talking in front of the altar in the church. No one knows how the quarrel started, but their angry meeting ended with Bruce stabbing Comyn, who died.

Scone Abbey on the Moot Hill.

The murder shocked everyone. Edward I called it treason and in a fury began to hunt Bruce down. The Comyns and their friends became Bruce's deadliest enemies. The Roman Church called it sacrilege and excommunicated Bruce. Bishop Wishart of Glasgow forgave Bruce, who promised to go on a crusade as soon as he was able. The bishop also told the people to support Bruce and produced robes for a coronation. With his supporters Bruce made his way to Perth and, at Scone Abbey a few weeks later, Robert Bruce was crowned king and became Robert I.

Bruce and his supporters, triumphant after his coronation.

27

# Bruce is Defeated and in Despair

Bruce did not have the trust and support of the community of the realm when he was crowned. He was seen as ambitious and rash. The murder of Comyn had divided the country. How could he beat the strongest king in Christendom when everyone else had failed? Edward I sent his army north 'to burn, slay and raise dragon'. No mercy was to be shown. Bruce's small army was destroyed by the heavy English cavalry at Methven near Perth in June 1306.

Bruce sent his queen, daughter and other royal ladies north to Kildrummy Castle, the strongest castle in Scotland. With a small group of friends he took to the hills on foot. In spite of great efforts

> *As outlaws went they many a day*
> *Among the hills, and fed on meat*
> *And water, nor had else to eat...*
> *Thus in the mountains wandered he*
> *Till most men in his companiy*
> *Were ragged and torn. They had, besides,*
> *No shoes but those they made of hides.*
>
> From the poem *The Brus* by John Barbour written in 1385

Edward did not catch Bruce, but he took revenge on his family. The women fleeing from attack at Kildrummy were captured at St Duthac's in Tain, where they had thought they were safe. Bruce's wife and daughter were imprisoned in nunneries after his daughter had spent some time in a cage in the Tower of London. His brother, Nigel, was executed. Bruce's sister, Mary, and the Countess of Buchan, who had crowned Bruce, were kept in cages outside the castle walls of Berwick and Roxburghe.

Kildrummy Castle was the strongest castle in the north.

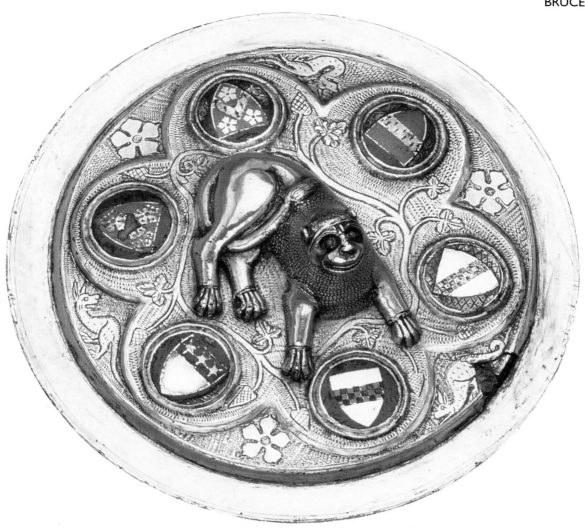

The lion surrounded by shields on the base of this drinking cup is said to represent Bruce surrounded by his supporters.

Two other brothers, Thomas and Alexander, were caught and executed. Bishops Wishart and Lamberton were imprisoned.

In the winter of 1306 Bruce stayed in the west with Celtic relatives and friends such as Christiana MacRuaridh of Garmoran and Angus Og MacDonald of Islay. These people always remained his friends and loyal supporters. When news of what had happened to his family came to him he must have wondered if the crown was worth the price his friends and relations were having to pay. Perhaps it was at this difficult time that Bruce took courage from a spider. Seeing a spider trying six times to swing its thread from one place to another and failing, Bruce said, 'I have been in six battles and failed. If the spider tries again and succeeds, I, too, will try again.' The spider tried again and succeeded. Bruce began to make plans.

# Civil War

With the help of his Celtic friends, Bruce landed on the Carrick coast. The Highland galleys brought him men from the west and supplies from Ireland.

This war was to be fought in a different way from before. They would not lay siege to castles or fight cavalry battles. This was 'secret war'. The soldiers were told to make hit-and-run raids to take the English by surprise. Wagons taking food to the castles were to be attacked. Crops to feed the English garrisons were to be destroyed. If a large army advanced against them they were to retreat into the forests.

When a castle was captured it was to be destroyed so that it could never be used against the Scots. Today we would call this a guerrilla war.

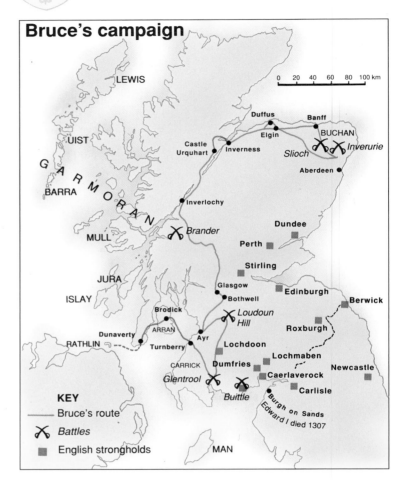

**Bruce's campaign**

Within a few weeks Bruce had ambushed cavalry in Glen Trool and cleared the way north. At Loudon Hill near Kilmarnock he forced the experienced English leader, Aylmer de Valence, to flee, then he defeated the Earl of Gloucester and his army.

Left: Bruce's Stone, Glen Trool. An English writer at the time said that, in spite of the terrible punishment for Scots supporting King Robert, 'the number of those willing to strengthen him in his kingship increased daily'.

Shortly after the defeat at Glen Trool (above) a Scots lord on the English side wrote, 'May it please God to prolong King Edward's life, for men say openly that when he is gone the victory will go to Bruce.'

On 7 July 1307 Edward I died on his way north. He wished his bones to be carried with the army until Bruce had been defeated, but his son, now King Edward II, went back to London. This was good news for Bruce. He moved north to attack the Comyns in Aberdeenshire and Moray. They were beaten and their lands destroyed so they could never again be a threat to Bruce.

Then the army went west to the MacDougalls of Argyll, allies of the Comyns and enemies of Bruce's Highland supporters. On the hillside above the Pass of Brander, the brilliant young James Douglas led a party of men who defeated the MacDougalls and forced their leaders to retreat to Edward II's court.

Bruce's only surviving brother, Edward, quickly brought Galloway under control in a harsh campaign. The Bruces had destroyed their enemies and the civil war was over. King Robert called a parliament in 1309. In two years he had built support for himself by his successful actions, but also because he had shown mercy to many of those who had once been against him.

31

cavalry battle. But they did have a year to make preparations.

# The Battle of Bannockburn

Edward II knew that he had to take action against the Scots. He called up an army from England, Ireland and Wales to relieve Stirling Castle. He had an army of around 2,000 cavalry and 15,000 foot soldiers (infantry). They greatly outnumbered the Scots.

King Robert had around 5,000 well-trained infantry and 500 fast-moving horsemen. The army had fought successfully under him and his captains for seven years, using guerrilla war tactics.

Above: This drawing from the fifteenth-century Scotichronicon shows Bruce killing Sir Henry de Bohun.

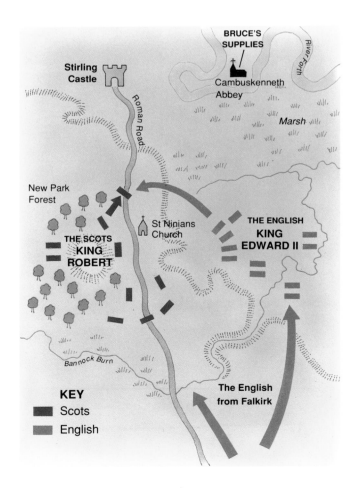

Left: A plan of the first day of the Battle of Bannockburn.

The Scots' spirits were high but their king knew a cavalry battle would be in Edward's favour. To help the Scots as much as possible, Bruce chose and prepared the battleground carefully. Ditches were dug and covered and small spikes called calthrops were scattered.

On 23 June 1314 the two armies faced each other. The English vanguard advanced against Bruce's battalion, which was blocking the road to Stirling. A young English knight, Sir Henry de Bohun, saw King Robert on his small grey pony. He charged him with his lance but Bruce killed him with one blow of his axe. Although the king's leaders called him foolish for risking his life in single combat his action had given his men confidence. They surged forward and beat the cavalry back.

Another English cavalry division left the main army. They crossed the Bannock Burn and, unseen, made for the rear of the Scots army. Bruce had placed Randolph's men to stop the Scots being out-flanked. Randolph's schiltrom advanced to meet the cavalry, who could not break the spearmen's bristling formation. Many horses and knights were killed but few Scots were harmed. The English retreated.

King Edward II led his army across the Bannock Burn and set up camp for the night. There was water for the horses but his army was hemmed in between streams running down to the River Forth, a short distance away.

In the night a Scots lord fighting for the English changed sides and encouraged Bruce to fight. At dawn the Scots' schiltroms advanced against the

**Brecbennach of St Columba was carried by the Scots into battle.**

cavalry. The horses had no room to move. The English could not use their strength and when Sir Robert Keith's horsemen scattered Edward's archers a Scots victory became possible. Edward fled the scene to prevent being captured. Many soldiers were drowned in the streams and River Forth trying to escape. Important prisoners were taken by the Scots and held to ransom.

# Good King Robert

Bruce had won the battle for his kingdom and he had the support of his people. Edward II was humiliated but he would not make peace. Bruce ransomed his prisoners of war for the return of his wife, daughter and friends held in England.

King Robert now faced two important tasks. He had to force the English to make peace and he had to rebuild his country. He sent his men to raid the north of England. They came back with money and goods paid to stop the Scots doing more damage. He sent an army to fight against the English in Ireland. His brother Edward was crowned King of Ireland but this campaign stopped when Edward was killed in 1318. In the same year Lord James Douglas won Berwick back from the English. Churchmen and lords were sent to the Pope to ask for his help to bring peace.

Trade in the burghs was encouraged to build up the country's wealth again. Some royal burghs like Aberdeen were rewarded for their loyalty. Burgesses represented the burghs at King Robert's parliaments. The churchmen, the nobles and the leaders of the towns again made up the three important groups of people helping to run the country.

The Church worked with the king. They put together the laws, called *Regiam Majestatem* (laws of the Kingdom), that Scotland was to use for the next 300 years. Bruce was a deeply religious man. He gave money and lands to the Church. He remembered his family who had died in the wars and had prayers said for them.

Since the start of the war with England the Pope, head of the Roman Catholic Church, had been important to both England and Scotland. In the time of Wallace, he had supported Scotland, but for most of the time he had been an ally of the English. The Scots sent many messengers and letters to the Pope in Rome. They wanted him to support Scotland and help stop the war.

After the murder of John Comyn by Bruce in 1306 the Pope excommunicated Bruce and his supporters. This meant he put them out of the Church and they were not allowed to take part in any holy services. This was a terrible punishment.

Above: The Seal of King Robert I followed a traditional pattern, with an armed knight on horseback on one side and the king giving out justice on the other.

Support for Bruce is declared on this tower at Dunfermline Abbey, where he is buried.

37

# The Declaration of Arbroath

The Scots churchmen who had helped Bruce to free Scotland found it very difficult being banned from the Church. They had to obey the Pope's orders, but they refused to help Edward II. The Scots tried to make the Pope change his mind.

To show their support for King Robert the leading nobles in the country signed a letter of protest and sent it to Pope John XXII. It was a declaration of the people's right to freedom and their duty to defend this right. The letter asked the Pope to accept the Scots' right to defend themselves against their more powerful, warlike neighbours, the English.

The letter, called the Declaration of Arbroath, said:

*'For it is not for glory, it is not riches, neither is it honour, but it is freedom alone that we fight and contend for, which no honest man will lose but with his life.'*

The declaration also stated that if Bruce should ever fail in his duty and accept English rule:

*'we will immediately endeavour to expel him as our enemy...and will make another King who will defend our liberties: for so long as there shall be but one hundred of us remain alive we will never give consent to subject ourselves to the dominion (rule) of the English.'*

The Declaration of Arbroath.

If the Pope refused to help, they said, God would hold him responsible for all the deaths and trouble still to come. The war between Scotland and England continued for several years in spite of the Declaration of Arbroath, and the Pope did not recognize Robert Bruce as King of Scotland until 1323. But Scotland's king had shown he was not only a great general but also a strong ruler. He had brought the different parts of the country together as one nation and shown himself to be a remarkable man.

Above: Scotland and England signed this peace treaty in Edinburgh in 1328.

The Declaration of Arbroath was drawn up at Arbroath Abbey. The abbot, Bernard of Linton, was in charge of drawing up letters to the Pope.

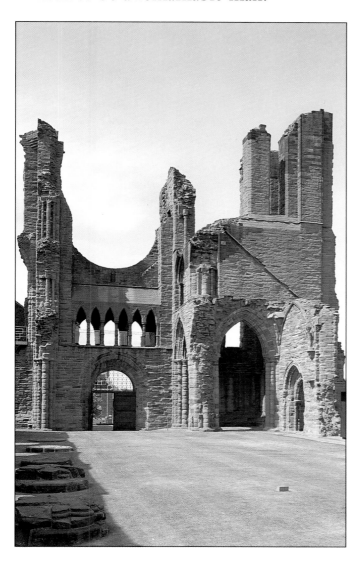

In 1328 Scotland and England finally signed a peace treaty in Edinburgh. But the English did not keep their promises to return the Stone of Destiny and other items Edward I stole from Scotland. In 1324 the nation welcomed an heir when Bruce's wife Queen Elizabeth gave birth to a son.

# The Bruce Legacy

At the end of his life Bruce could look back on a long struggle to free the country from the English and to be accepted as King of Scots by other nations. The old Celtic earldoms of Scotland remained and Bruce gave them to his supporters as rewards for their loyalty.

The families of Douglas, Murray and the Stewarts joined the Bruces as the biggest landholders in Scotland. Families like the Comyns and Baliols were never to be as powerful again. The loyal MacDonalds, the Lords of the Isles, controlled much of the west. Bruce's daughter, Marjory, had a son who was the first Stewart king and, much later (in 1603), the Stewarts brought together Scotland and England under one king, James VI of Scotland and I of England.

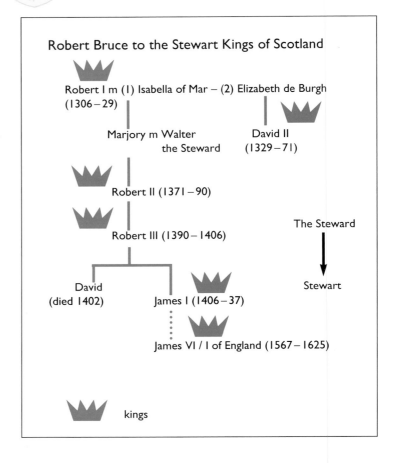

Robert Bruce to the Stewart Kings of Scotland

Robert I m (1) Isabella of Mar – (2) Elizabeth de Burgh (1306–29)

Marjory m Walter the Steward

David II (1329–71)

Robert II (1371–90)

Robert III (1390–1406)

The Steward

Stewart

David (died 1402)

James I (1406–37)

James VI / I of England (1567–1625)

kings

**The famous statue of King Robert I at Bannockburn Heritage Centre.**

The struggle against England had helped three groups of people to become important in the running of the country: the Church, the nobles and the burgesses of the growing towns.

Warfare had changed during these years. The Scots had shown how mobile, well trained spearmen could defeat a heavy cavalry force. Archers became very important in battles, attacking from a safe distance. Fast, mounted soldiers, like Bruce's raiding parties, proved difficult to beat and became more important than the heavily armoured knights on warhorses.

In the later years of his reign Bruce spent time in a new home in the west at Cardross. He did not build a castle but a manor house, and a galley to sail the western islands. His life had been full of ambition when he was young but as a king he was also generous to his friends, merciful to his enemies and careful to protect his country.

This skull from Dunfermline Abbey is thought to be of Robert the Bruce. It was used by the sculptor Pilkington Jackson to make the likeness on the opposite page.

### Scots Wha Hae

Scots, wha hae wi' Wallace bled,
Scots, wham Bruce has aften led,
Welcome to your gory bed,
                Or to victorie!

Now's the day, and now's the hour:
See the front o' battle lour,
See approach proud Edward's power -
                Chains and slaverie!

Wha will be a traitor knave?
Wha can fill a coward's grave?
Wha sae base as be a slave? -
                Let him turn, and flee!

Wha for Scotland's King and Law
Freedom's sword will strongly draw,
Freeman stand or freeman fa',
                Let him follow me!

By Oppression's woes and pains,
By your sons in servile chains,
We will drain our dearest veins
                But they shall be free!

Lay the proud usurpers low!
Tyrants fall in every foe!
Liberty's in every blow!
                Let us do, or die!

Robert Burns, 1759-96

Wallace and Bruce are remembered in some of the earliest written Scots poetry: *The Brus*, written in 1375 and Blind Harry's *The Wallace*, composed in the fifteenth century. The community of the realm, the people of Scotland, had fought together against a foreign invader. The Highlanders and the Lowlanders had been brought together by Bruce to fight for the same cause. The wars with England were to carry on for many more years. Battles were lost and won, but Scotland's future as a separate nation was secure.

# Glossary

**Allies** People who support you in a war.

**Ambushed** Made a surprise attack.

**Archers** Soldiers who used bows and arrows.

**Bailiwicks** Areas for which an official is responsible.

**Burgesses** The most important people who lived in the burghs.

**Calthrops** Small weapons with four spikes that always had one spike facing up, however they landed. Battle fields were spread with them to injure the horses and cause confusion.

**Cavalry** Soldiers on horseback.

**Chain mail** A kind of armour made from links of metal.

**Christendom** Those countries that were Christian in belief.

**Community of the realm** The groups of people who made up the country.

**Conscripts** Soldiers who were forced to join the army.

**Crusade** A war fought by Christians to win back the Holy Land from Muslims in the Middle Ages.

**Earls** The most important nobles. Scotland had about thirteen earls.

**Galley** An open boat that used both sails and oars.

**Garrisons** The soldiers who guarded a castle.

**Grappling hook** A hook on the end of a rope. It is thrown over a wall to help climb up it.

**Guardians** People who were chosen to run the country when there was no king.

**Guilds** Groups of traders who helped each other.

**Heir** Someone who will take a title when the person who holds it dies, such as a prince becoming king when his father the king dies.

**Homage** A show of respect or honour to someone.

**Inglis** An early form of the English language.

**Looted** Stole.

**Mace** A metal or metal-headed war club, often with spikes.

**Middle Ages** A name given to the time in history between 500 and 1500 AD.

**Missionaries** People who moved around the country spreading their religious beliefs.

**Pilgrimage** A journey to a holy place.

**Portcullis** A gate that can be lowered to close an entrance to a castle.

**Ransom** A price paid to free a prisoner.

**Religious orders** The different groups of monks and nuns.

**Sacrilege** A crime against the Church.

**Saxons** The people who lived in England before the Norman Conquest.

**Schiltrom** A company of spearmen closely packed together in a circle, with their spears pointing outwards.

**Siege engine** A machine that attacked castles by firing stones at them.

**Tolls** Payments for the use of something, such as a road or a mill.

**Touns** Small groups of houses in farming communities.

**Traditions** Beliefs and ways of doing things handed down from one generation to the next.

**Treason** Betraying your country.

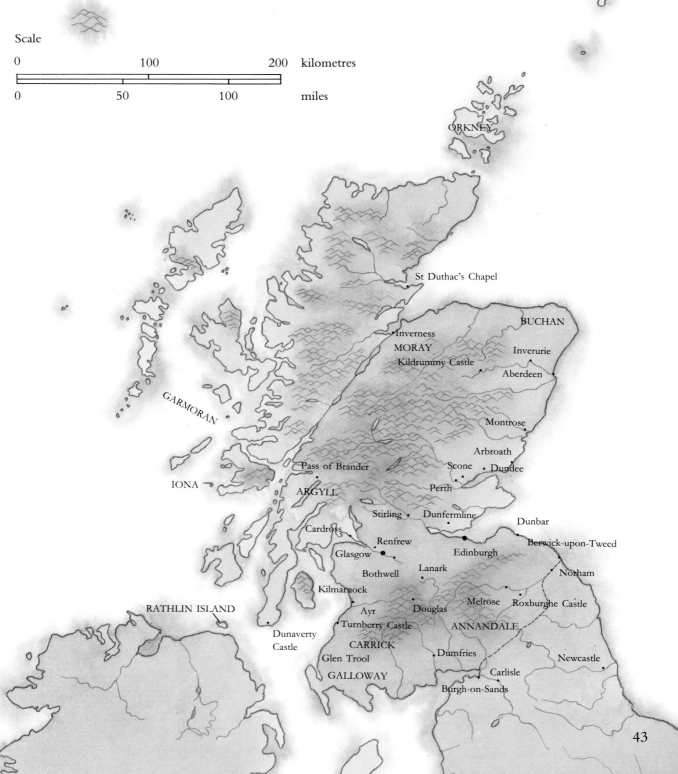

**A map of Scotland, including places mentioned in the text.**

Scale

| 0 | 100 | 200 | kilometres |
| 0 | 50 | 100 | miles |

SHETLAND

ORKNEY

St Duthac's Chapel

BUCHAN

Inverness

MORAY

Inverurie

Kildrummy Castle

Aberdeen

GARMORAN

Montrose

Arbroath

Pass of Brander

Scone · Dundee

IONA

Perth

ARGYLL

Stirling · Dunfermline

Dunbar

Cardross

Renfrew

Berwick-upon-Tweed

Glasgow

Edinburgh

Bothwell

Lanark

Norham

Kilmarnock

Melrose · Roxburghe Castle

RATHLIN ISLAND

Ayr · Douglas

Turnberry Castle

ANNANDALE

Newcastle

Dunaverty
Castle

CARRICK

Dumfries

Glen Trool

Carlisle

GALLOWAY

Burgh-on-Sands

43

# Further Information

## Books to read

**Non fiction:**
Some history books give information on Scotland as well as England at this time or the information is suitable to both countries.
*Norman Britain* by Tony Triggs (Wayland, 1990). A good general picture of the Normans.
*History Makers of the Middle Ages* by Peter Chrisp (Wayland, 1994). Includes a chapter on Robert Bruce.
*Robert the Bruce, King of Scots* by Ronald McNair Scott (Canongate Press, 1988)

**Fiction:**
*Quest for a Maid* by Frances Mary Hendry (Canongate Press, 1988)
A story of people in the burghs at the time of the death of Alexander III.

## Places to visit

Bannockburn Heritage Centre run by National Trust for Scotland
Wallace Monument run by Stirling District Council
Glen Trool Visitor Centre, Glen Trool
Scottish Abbeys and Castles – many are run by Historic Scotland, who produce guide books. Historic Scotland also produce good packs of information on many historic places such as Arbroath Abbey and Stirling Castle.
There are often local references to the Wars of Independence around the country. Museums and maps are good starting points to find out more.

BBC Education Scotland have produced the following two units of programmes on this topic (transmissions Autumn 1994):
For TV – *Bruce's Scotland* in *Around Scotland* (also made in Gaelic).
For radio – *Wallace's Scotland* in *Scottish Resources* 10–12.
Print support is available from: BBC Education, 5 Queen Street, Edinburgh EH2 1JF.

# Index